# ULTIMATE
# **MLB**
## Road Trip

By Bo Mitchell

**ULTIMATE SPORTS**
**ROAD TRIPS**

SportsZone

An Imprint of Abdo Publishing
abdobooks.com

# ABDOBOOKS.COM

Published by Abdo Publishing, a division of ABDO, PO Box 398166, Minneapolis, Minnesota 55439. Copyright © 2019 by Abdo Consulting Group, Inc. International copyrights reserved in all countries. No part of this book may be reproduced in any form without written permission from the publisher. SportsZone™ is a trademark and logo of Abdo Publishing.

Printed in the United States of America, North Mankato, Minnesota
092018
012019

THIS BOOK CONTAINS
RECYCLED MATERIALS

Cover Photo: Brandon Sloter/AP Images
Interior Photos: Brandon Sloter/AP Images, 1; Stan Szeto/Cal Sport Media/AP Images, 4–5; Douglas Peebles/Corbis/Splash News/Newscom, 7; John Hefti/Icon Sportswire/AP Images, 9; Douglas Stringer/ Icon Sportswire/AP Images, 10; Hans Blossey/Image Broker/Rex Features, 13; Jayne Kamin–Oncea/Getty Images Sport/Getty Images, 14; Dilip Vishwanat/Getty Images Sport/Getty Images, 17; Joe Robbins/ Getty Images Sport/Getty Images, 18, 26–27, 40–41, 44; Steven Bergerson/Major League Baseball/ Getty Images, 21; Frank Romeo/Shutterstock Images, 22; Paul Beaty/AP Images, 25; Aero–Imaging, Inc/ Newscom, 29; Focus On Sport/Getty Images Sport/Getty Images, 30; Alfredo Garcia Saz/Shutterstock Images, 33, 45; Brandon Sloter/AP Images, 34–35; Julie Jacobson/AP Images, 36; Billie Weiss/Boston Red Sox/Getty Images Sport/Getty Images, 39; Heinz Kluetmeier/Sports Illustrated/Getty Images, 42

Editor: Bradley Cole
Series Designer: Melissa Martin

**Library of Congress Cataloging-in-Publication Data: 2018949187**

**Publisher's Cataloging-in-Publication Data**

Names: Mitchell, Bo, author.
Title: Ultimate MLB road trip / by Bo Mitchell.
Description: Minneapolis, Minnesota : Abdo Publishing, 2019 | Series: Ultimate sports road trips | Includes online resources and index.
Identifiers: ISBN 9781532117527 (lib. bdg.) | ISBN 9781532170386 (ebook)
Subjects: LCSH: Sports arenas--Juvenile literature. | Sports spectators--Juvenile literature. | Baseball-- Juvenile literature. | Major League Baseball Enterprises--Juvenile literature.
Classification: DDC 796.357068--dc23

# TABLE OF CONTENTS

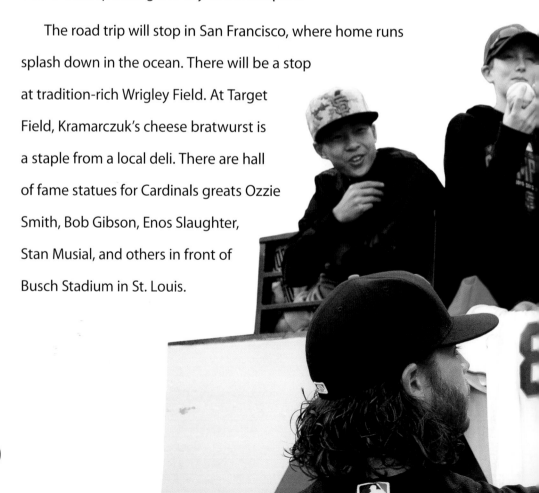

# INTRO

# **Take Me Out**
## TO THE BALL GAME!

The ultimate baseball road trip will visit the most impressive and historic stadiums in Major League Baseball (MLB). From delicious food to great traditions and loyal fans, there is nothing better than spending the day at the ballpark.

The road trip will stop in San Francisco, where home runs splash down in the ocean. There will be a stop at tradition-rich Wrigley Field. At Target Field, Kramarczuk's cheese bratwurst is a staple from a local deli. There are hall of fame statues for Cardinals greats Ozzie Smith, Bob Gibson, Enos Slaughter, Stan Musial, and others in front of Busch Stadium in St. Louis.

From Chavez Ravine to the Green Monster, and all points in between, these venues offer the best experiences for fans of the great game of baseball.

Baseball parks provide some of the best experiences for fans in all of sports.

# AT&T PARK

The first stop of the Ultimate MLB Road Trip is out west in San Francisco. AT&T Park has been the home of the San Francisco Giants since the turn of the century. It's the only sports stadium in the city. From the park you can see San Francisco Bay, the downtown skyline, and the San Francisco-Oakland Bay Bridge.

This stadium is filled with great things to see and do. Just past the right field wall at AT&T Park is a body of water called China Basin. It's part of San Francisco Bay. Giants fans call China Basin "McCovey Cove" after Willie McCovey, the slugging first baseman who debuted with the Giants in 1959 and retired in 1980. He is one of the best to ever play for the Giants and is in the National Baseball Hall of Fame. McCovey batted left-handed, so if he would have played at AT&T Park, his long home runs to right field would have landed in the water. That's why the bay is named after him. Next to McCovey Cove stands a statue of the great player.

# AT&T PARK

## San Francisco, California

**Date Opened:** April 11, 2000
**Capacity:** 41,915
**Home Team:** San Francisco Giants

Families gather in a park next to the water to play catch, take batting practice, or walk along the shore.

McCovey isn't the only player honored at AT&T Park. The Giants' Wall of Fame features plaques that honor many of the other great players in team history, such as 1960s greats Willie Mays and Juan Marichal. One of those legends is Barry Bonds. In just the second year of AT&T Park, Bonds hit a major league record 73 home runs. The last one sailed over the right field fence at AT&T Park. Six years later, he broke the record books with the 756th home run of his career. He swatted that one at AT&T Park, too.

Beyond the left field wall, the Fan Lot is open to anyone with a ticket to the game. It includes a place to run the bases and go down four special slides. Kids marvel at the giant old-fashioned baseball glove statue and the Coca-Cola Superslide with a huge bottle at the top. The huge Coca-Cola bottle

## FUN FACT

Sometimes home run balls splash down in McCovey Cove. Fans on boats and rafts float in the cove during the game, waiting for a ball. Some bring giant nets to scoop up their prize. Some just dive in the water and swim after the baseballs.

With features such as McCovey Cove, a giant baseball glove, and a Coca-Cola bottle slide, AT&T Park is a hit with fans of all ages.

Superslide lights up when a Giants player hits a home run. The bottle is 47 feet (14 m) tall and weighs 130,000 pounds (59,000 kg).

AT&T Park has received many awards for recycling and composting. Solar panels in several places around the stadium power buildings and homes in the area. Two restaurants use

fresh ingredients from the Garden, an area in the park where children can learn with hands-on activities about garden beds and aeroponics towers. AT&T Park has even won awards for its conservation. It has won the MLB Green Glove Award for most environmentally friendly stadium nine-straight times.

Through 2018 the Giants had reached the World Series four times since AT&T Park opened. They won three championships—in 2010, 2012, and 2014. They have never clinched the World Series at AT&T, but their home-field advantage is strong. The Giants are 8–2 in World Series games there.

Former Giants ace Juan Marichal was honored with a statue outside AT&T Park.

# DODGER
## STADIUM

D odger Stadium is one of the most beautiful ballparks in the country, with palm trees and mountains in the background. On days when there isn't a Los Angeles Dodgers game, anyone can bring a lunch into Dodger Stadium, climb the steps to the top deck, and eat there, just to enjoy the great view. It's free.

The stadium is sometimes referred to as "Chavez Ravine" for the name of the neighborhood where it was built. In 2009 the US Postal Service made Dodger Stadium the first stadium with its own ZIP code. The stadium and the area around it—known as "Dodgertown, USA"—have the ZIP code 90090.

Dodger Stadium has seen its share of history. Some of the game's greatest players and

## FUN FACT

Umbrellas are not allowed into Dodger Stadium. But going into the 2018 season only 17 games had been rained out in Dodger Stadium history. The last rainout was April 17, 2000.

# DODGER STADIUM

## Los Angeles, California

**Date Opened:** April 10, 1962
**Capacity:** 56,000
**Home Team:** Los Angeles Dodgers

most interesting characters have called it home through the years. In 2017 the stadium hosted its ninth World Series, as the home team fell to the Houston Astros in seven games.

One of the most famous moments in stadium history came during Game 1 of the 1988 World Series between the Dodgers and

 The San Gabriel Mountains provide a picturesque backdrop for Dodgers home games.

the Oakland A's. The A's led 4–3 in the bottom of the ninth inning. With two outs and a runner on first base, Kirk Gibson limped to the plate as a pinch hitter. The Los Angeles slugger didn't start the game because of injuries to both legs. Then the runner on first stole second base. With the count full and a runner on second, Gibson lined a slider over the wall in right field to win the game. As Gibson hobbled around the bases, legendary CBS announcer Jack Buck exclaimed, "I don't believe what I just saw!"

## FUN FACT

Dodger Stadium sells more hot dogs than any ballpark in baseball. Approximately 2.5 million of the famous "Dodger Dogs" are gobbled up by Los Angeles baseball fans each year.

Thirty years later, Gibson autographed the seat where the famous home run landed. Gibson had been diagnosed with Parkinson's disease in 2015. The Dodgers decided to donate the money raised by selling tickets for his home run seat and the one next to it to the Parkinson's Research Center.

# BUSCH
## STADIUM

After 40 years at Busch Memorial Stadium, the St. Louis Cardinals moved into a brand-new home with a similar name. Busch Stadium is sometimes called "The New Busch Stadium" or "Busch Stadium III" to tell it apart from the former stadiums. A great view of downtown St. Louis, including the famous Gateway Arch, makes this another one of the most beautiful ballparks in the country.

The Cardinals felt at home right away in their new ballpark. They won the World Series in that very first season in 2006 and won it again in 2011. Both championships were clinched at Busch Stadium. In between those two titles, the stadium also hosted the 80th MLB All-Star Game in 2009.

**FUN FACT**

The 2006 Cardinals became the first team since the 1923 New York Yankees to win a championship in its first year playing in a new stadium.

# BUSCH STADIUM

## St. Louis, Missouri

**Date Opened:** April 10, 2006
**Capacity:** 45,538
**Home Team:** St. Louis Cardinals

 Despite being a new stadium, Busch Stadium is packed with history.

The Cardinals have been around for more than 100 years. Their

11 World Series titles rank No. 1 among National League teams

and second only to the New York Yankees overall. Baseball history runs deep in St. Louis, and fans can learn all about it at the Ballpark Village just beyond the outfield walls of Busch Stadium. The Cardinals Hall of Fame and Museum fills the second floor of Ballpark Village. Stan Musial slugged his way into Cardinals history, and a statue commemorates "Stan the Man" outside the third-base entrance of the stadium. Statues of other Hall of Famers who played for the Cardinals, such as Ozzie Smith and Bob Gibson, also stand just outside the park.

## FUN FACT

On the first Opening Day at Busch Stadium in 2006, Albert Pujols hit the first home run by a Cardinals player at the new ballpark. Pujols went on to hit 48 more homers that year.

The Cardinals support a number of Earth-friendly initiatives at Busch Stadium. Visitors will notice more than 500 recycling bins spread throughout the stadium. Volunteers also collect recycling every game. Members of the "Green Team" walk through the aisles gathering recyclable material between innings and get to watch the games for free. It's one of many programs that make Busch Stadium one of the greenest ballparks in the country.

# **TARGET**
## FIELD

After playing their first 21 seasons at suburban Metropolitan Stadium, the Minnesota Twins spent 28 years indoors at the Hubert H. Humphrey Metrodome. But in 2010 the team returned to its roots, moving into a shiny new home across town where fans could once again watch baseball played on real grass under blue skies. Target Field is the newest stadium on the road trip.

The limestone walls of Target Field give the stadium an outdoor Minnesota look and feel. And the Twins actually brought a big piece of their first stadium to their new home. The tallest of the three flagpoles standing on the right field plaza was first used at Metropolitan Stadium. When the Twins

# TARGET FIELD

## Minneapolis, Minnesota

**Date Opened:** April 12, 2010
**Capacity:** 39,504
**Home Team:** Minnesota Twins

left "the Met" in 1981, the old flagpole was moved to nearby Richfield, Minnesota, where it stood outside the American Legion building until being relocated to Target Field in 2010.

 Since 2010 the Twins have shown off a ballpark that is one of the most environmentally friendly in the country.

The Twins support the environment by reusing the rain water that falls on Target Field. When it rains, water is collected under the stadium and is used later to water the outfield grass or wash the grandstands. This helps save more than 2 million gallons (7.5 million L) of water each year.

One of Target Field's highlights was the 85th MLB All-Star Game, played in 2014. The American League won the game, which will be remembered as Derek Jeter's final All-Star appearance. Twins pitcher Glen Perkins got the final three outs with teammate Kurt Suzuki behind the plate. It was the third All-Star Game played in Minnesota. The Metrodome hosted it in 1985 and the Met had the game in 1965.

## FUN FACT

The Target Field flagpole that waves the US flag was 90 feet (27 m) tall and weighed almost two tons (1,800 kg) when it stood at Metropolitan Stadium. After being moved twice and cut down, it's now only half the size.

# 5 WRIGLEY FIELD

Staying in the Midwest, the road trip takes us to the north side of Chicago—to the second-oldest stadium in baseball and the oldest park in the National League. Wrigley Field opened as the home of the Federal League's Chicago Whales in 1914. The Federal League folded after 1915, so the Chicago Cubs moved in, and they've played their home games in the "friendly confines" ever since.

## FUN FACT

Wrigley Field is named after William Wrigley Jr., the founder of the Wrigley chewing gum company. He took over as the owner of the Cubs in 1918 and changed the name of the ballpark from Cubs Park to Wrigley Field in 1926.

Wrigley Field is famous for its old-fashioned charm, including the ivy vines that cover the brick outfield walls. The ivy hasn't always been there. It was planted in 1937. If a batted ball gets lost in the ivy, it's considered a ground-rule double. The original hand-operated scoreboard is as old as the ivy and is still in use.

# WRIGLEY FIELD

## Chicago, Illinois

**Date Opened:** April 23, 1914
**Capacity:** 41,649
**Home Team:** Chicago Cubs

 **Features such as the ivy and classic scoreboard help make Wrigley Field unique among ballparks.**

Sitting 490 feet (149 m) from home plate, the scoreboard has never been hit by a batted ball.

Wrigley was the last MLB stadium to install lights. Before 1988 a city ordinance prevented the Cubs from playing night games at home. Originally, residents of "Wrigleyville" didn't want the stadium lights on at night while people tried to sleep. But after pressure from the team and MLB, the city relented. Wrigley Field hosted its first night game on August 8, 1988. The Cubs still play the most daytime home games in the league.

The neighborhood around the stadium is a circus of activity on game days. It's filled with restaurants for fans to enjoy before and after Cubs games. Buildings across the street from Wrigley Field sell seats on the roofs where fans can see into the stadium and watch the game.

Some great moments in baseball history have taken place at Wrigley Field, including the famous "Called Shot" by Yankees slugger Babe Ruth during the 1932 World Series. According to legend, Ruth pointed toward center field during an at-bat and then hit the next pitch to that spot for a home run.

# 6 ORIOLE PARK
## AT CAMDEN YARDS

The home of the Baltimore Orioles changed the way new baseball stadiums looked. Until Oriole Park at Camden Yards opened, most stadiums were designed to accommodate football and baseball. The new ballpark at Camden Yards was made only for baseball and designed to look old-fashioned. It was the first modern stadium designed to remind fans of how ballparks used to look in the sport's Golden Era. Its retro appearance set a trend still being followed.

## FUN FACT

Babe Ruth was born in Baltimore, just two blocks from where Oriole Park at Camden Yards opened 97 years later. When he was older, Ruth and his family lived in a building located where center field of the ballpark sits today.

One of the most noticeable features about the ballpark is the eight-story brick warehouse across Eutaw Street beyond right field. It was built in 1899 as a warehouse for Baltimore and

# ORIOLE PARK AT CAMDEN YARDS

## Baltimore, Maryland

**Date Opened:** April 6, 1992
**Capacity:** 45,971
**Home Team:** Baltimore Orioles

Ohio Railroad, which ran a terminal called Camden Yards at the site. That's where the ballpark got its name. Many sluggers have hit home runs onto Eutaw Street, but nobody has ever hit the B&O building on the fly during a game.

 **Cal Ripken played his way into the record book at Camden Yards.**

Plaques honoring former Orioles players can be found inside the center field gate along Eutaw Street. Two of those Orioles greats made history at Camden Yards just one year apart.

Orioles shortstop Cal Ripken Jr. played in his 2,131st

consecutive game on September 6, 1995. That broke the amazing record Lou Gehrig set 56 years earlier. He also hit a home run that night. Fans attending the historic game gave him a standing ovation once the game became official. Fireworks shot from behind the scoreboard. Confetti fluttered down to the cheering fans and the field. Ripken took a victory lap around the field and shook hands with fans in the front rows.

Exactly one year later, Orioles first baseman Eddie Murray swatted the 500th home run of his great career. Murray became just the third player ever with 3,000 hits and 500 homers in his career. The other two? Hank Aaron and Willie Mays, putting Murray in elite company.

# 7

# YANKEE
## STADIUM

Baseball's most famous team has one of its newest stadiums. Building Yankee Stadium cost $1.5 billion. The home of the New York Yankees is the most expensive baseball stadium in the world and it's the next-to-last stop on the ultimate baseball road trip.

The Yankees played at the original Yankee Stadium from 1923 until 1973. It closed for a few years for renovations before once again hosting Yankees games from 1976 to 2008. It was nicknamed "The House that Ruth Built" after the great Babe Ruth. Many of the greatest Yankees players were honored with monuments to honor them beyond center field at the old ballpark. The team moved those monuments to the new stadium, where they are proudly

## FUN FACT

The Yankees honored 22 former players and managers by retiring their jersey numbers, which are displayed in Monument Park. No. 1 through No. 10 are all retired, so no Yankee will ever wear a single-digit number on his jersey again.

# YANKEE STADIUM

## Bronx, New York

**Date Opened:** April 2, 2009
**Capacity:** 52,325
**Home Team:** New York Yankees

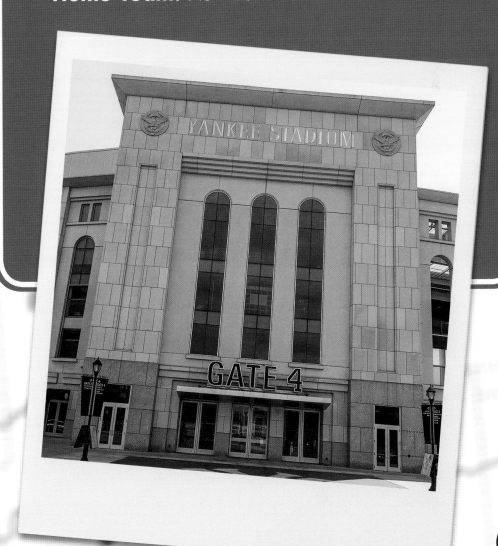

**Many parts of the new stadium help make it feel like home for the Yankees.**

displayed in Monument Park beyond the center field wall. Fans

can pay tribute to Ruth, Lou Gehrig, Joe DiMaggio, Yogi Berra, and

other greats before the start of games.

The current Yankee Stadium was designed to look a lot like the

old stadium. The outside wall is still made of limestone and granite

and the roof has white lattice, just like the old stadium. The new

Yankee Stadium even has the same dimensions as the original Yankee Stadium. And the bullpens are in the same place.

Not everything about the new ballpark was patterned after its predecessor, however. The huge scoreboard in center field was the third-biggest high-definition scoreboard in the world when Yankee Stadium opened. It measures 59 by 101 feet (18 by 31 m).

The new Yankee Stadium has already been home to some memorable baseball moments involving newer Yankee greats. The Yankees won their 27th World Series in 2009 in the first year

 Derek Jeter's last game was one of the most memorable moments in the new Yankee Stadium.

of Yankee Stadium. They also won the World Series in 1923, the first year of the original Yankee Stadium.

Mariano Rivera took the mound at Yankee Stadium for the final time of his 19-year career on September 26, 2013. Rivera is considered the best relief pitcher of all time. When he was done, the tearful Rivera came out of the game to an incredible ovation.

And in his final game at Yankee Stadium on September 25, 2014, Derek Jeter smashed a single to right field to knock in the winning run and give his Yankees the win. After the game, Jeter ended his 20-year career by walking back out to his spot at shortstop, waving to the cheering fans.

Fans should come hungry to Yankee Stadium. Concessions include multiple "build your own nachos" locations. Bareburger brings bison burgers and veggie options to the plate. And for those with a sweet tooth, the Yankees-themed Grand Slam Shake should hit the spot.

# FENWAY
## PARK

The final stop of our trip takes us to the oldest stadium in baseball. Fenway Park was built more than 100 years ago. Some of the greatest stars in baseball history have played there. It was added to the National Register of Historic Places in 2012.

Fenway Park features quirky outfield corners and the smallest amount of foul territory in baseball. Its best-known feature is "the Green Monster," the wall in left field that stands 37 feet (11 m) high. It sits just 310 feet (94 m) from home plate, guarding against cheap home runs. The Monster intercepts many long drives that would easily reach the seats in most ballparks, usually leaving the hitter to settle for a double. But the Monster also turns a lot of high, short

## FUN FACT

Like the Yankees at Yankee Stadium and Cardinals at Busch Stadium, the Red Sox won the World Series in their first season at Fenway Park, back in 1912.

# FENWAY PARK

## Boston, Massachusetts

**Date Opened:** April 20, 1912
**Capacity:** 37,731
**Home Team:** Boston Red Sox

 The Green Monster is a famous part of the charm of Fenway Park.

fly balls into home runs, making Fenway a house of horrors for left-handed pitchers.

The left-field pole next to the Green Monster is called "Fisk Pole" after former Red Sox catcher Carlton Fisk. In Game 6 of the 1975 World Series, Fisk hit a drive off that pole over the Green Monster. Fisk hopped down the first-base line waving his arms,

urging the ball to stay fair. It did, and his homer won the game for Boston. It's one of the most famous home runs in baseball history.

Across the field, the foul pole in right field is listed at 302 feet (92 m) away from home plate, making it the shortest in the majors. And many have argued that distance is actually closer to 295 feet (90 m). It's nicknamed "Pesky's Pole" after former Red Sox player

Johnny Pesky. Right field doesn't require a high wall, however, as it quickly drops back to a depth of 380 feet (116 m).

In 2004 the Red Sox won the World Series for the first time in 86 years, ending the "Curse of the Bambino." The curse was a superstition that many Red Sox fans believed. Their team sold Babe Ruth (the Bambino) to the Yankees following the 1919 season. It turned out to be a terrible deal that haunted the Red Sox for a long time. The first two games of the 2004 World Series were won by the Red Sox at Fenway before they clinched it with two more wins over the Cardinals in St. Louis.

## FUN FACT

The Green Monster was made of wood in 1912. In 1934, it was covered in tin and concrete, and a scoreboard was added to the base of the fence. It was painted green in 1947. The team added seating above the Monster in 2003.

Three years later, they swept the Colorado Rockies in the World Series, again winning the first two games at Fenway. The Red Sox finally celebrated a world championship at home in 2013, clinching the title against the Cardinals on October 30, 2013, in front of their home fans.

**The Red Sox were undefeated at Fenway in both the 2004 and 2007 World Series.**

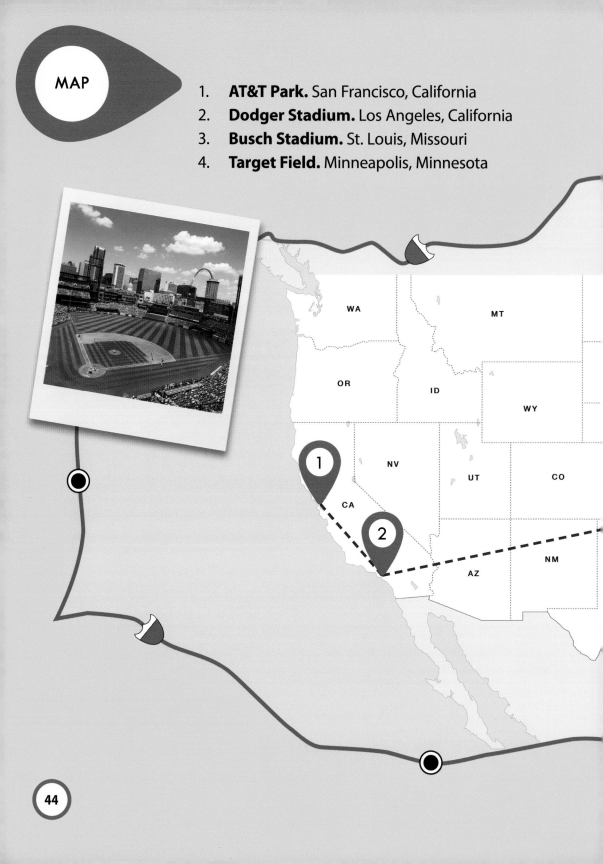

# MAP

1. **AT&T Park.** San Francisco, California
2. **Dodger Stadium.** Los Angeles, California
3. **Busch Stadium.** St. Louis, Missouri
4. **Target Field.** Minneapolis, Minnesota

WA

MT

OR

ID

WY

NV

UT

CO

CA

1

2

NM

AZ

5. **Wrigley Field.** Chicago, Illinois
6. **Oriole Park at Camden Yards.** Baltimore, Maryland
7. **Yankee Stadium.** Bronx, New York
8. **Fenway Park.** Boston, Massachusetts

# Glossary

**capacity**

The number of seats for fans in a stadium.

**clinched**

Finalized a series victory, division title, or wild card spot.

**dimensions**

The measurements of a baseball field down the foul lines and to the outfield wall.

**grandstands**

The main seating areas in a stadium.

**lattice**

Strips of wood or metal attached with diamond shapes in between to make a fence.

**meteorologist**

A scientist who studies the weather.

**ordinance**

A rule made by a city or county.

**ovation**

Long applause by an audience, usually done while standing.

**rainout**

Cancellation of a game due to rain.

**renovations**

Repairs made to a building.

**retro**

Imitating the past style of something, such as a building.

# More Information

## BOOKS

Holub, Joan. *Who Was Babe Ruth?* New York: Grosset & Dunlap, 2012.

Jacobs, Greg. *The Everything Kids' Baseball Book*. Avon, MA: Adams Media, 2018.

Kortemeier, Todd. *Total Baseball*. Minneapolis, MN: Abdo Publishing, 2017.

# Online Resources

To learn more about MLB ballparks, visit **abdobooklinks.com**. These links are routinely monitored and updated to provide the most current information available.

# Index

# About the Author

Following his lifelong passion, Bo Mitchell began writing about sports professionally in 1993. He has lived in Minnesota his entire life and graduated from the University of Minnesota in Minneapolis. Bo has worked in sports radio and his writing has appeared on many websites as well as in magazines and newspapers. He grew up in the Minneapolis suburb of Richfield, Minnesota, and during the summer as a kid he could hear the stadium announcer at Metropolitan Stadium from his back yard during Twins games.